duke elling

Arranged by Brent Edstrom

Front cover photo by Photo by Michael Ochs Archives/Getty Images

ISBN 978-1-4234-5914-9

HAL•LEONARD®
CORPORATION

7777 W. BLUEMOUND RD. P.O. BOX 13819 MILWAUKEE, WI 53213

Visit Hal Leonard Online at
www.halleonard.com

C-JAM BLUES

By DUKE ELLINGTON

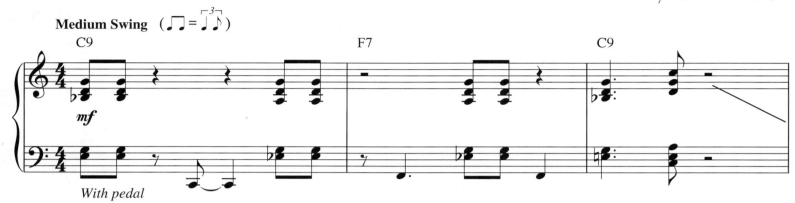

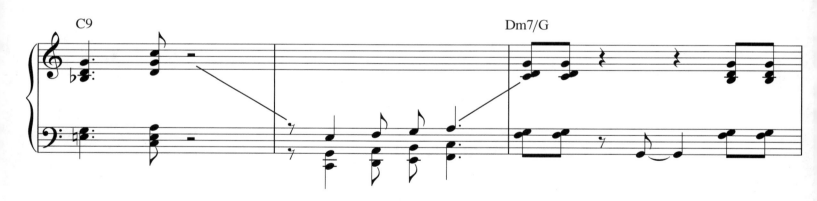

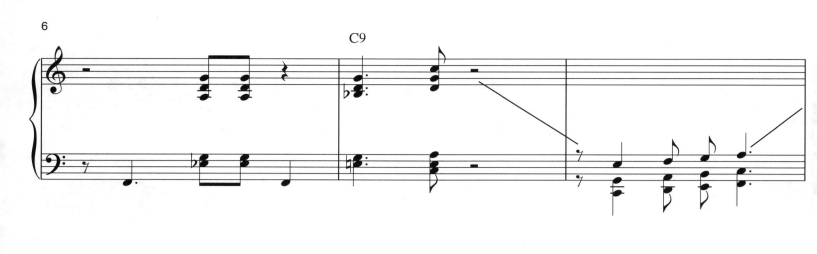

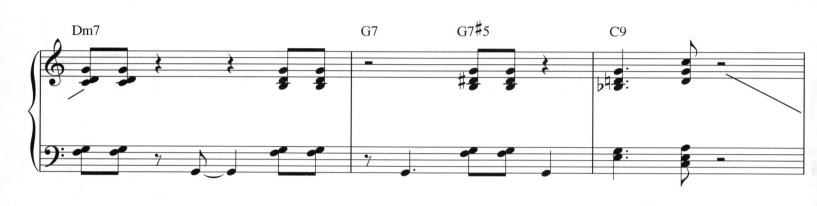

CARAVAN
from SOPHISTICATED LADIES

Words and Music by DUKE ELLINGTON,
IRVING MILLS and JUAN TIZOL

Bright Afro-Latin

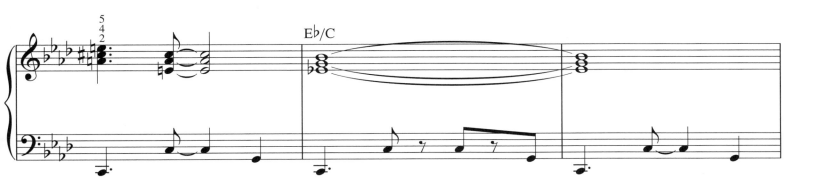

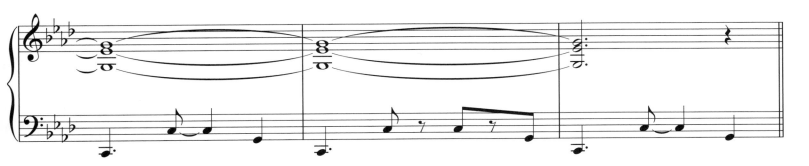

8

COME SUNDAY
from BLACK, BROWN & BEIGE

By DUKE ELLINGTON

DANCERS IN LOVE

By DUKE ELLINGTON

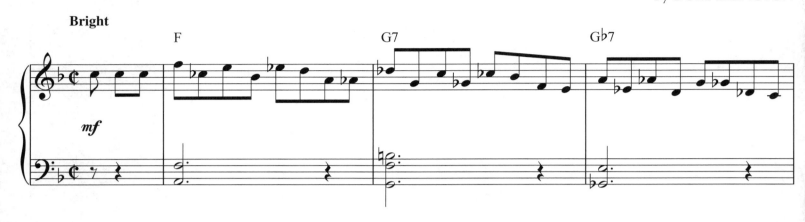

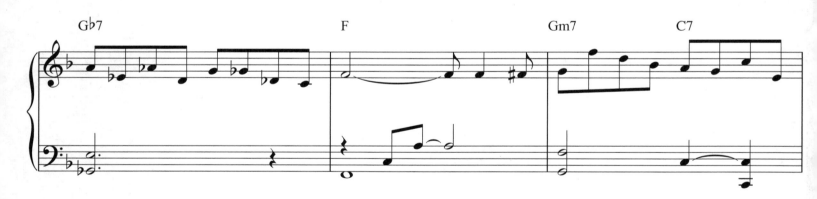

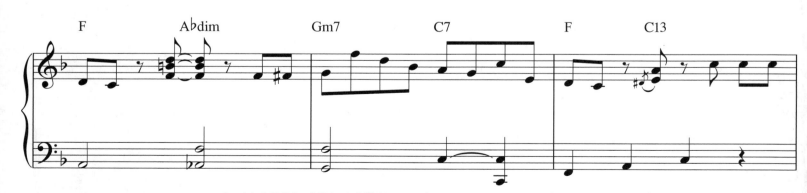

I'M JUST A LUCKY SO AND SO

Words by MACK DAVID
Music by DUKE ELLINGTON

Very slow and rhythmical

'DO NOTHIN' TILL YOU HEAR FROM ME

Words and Music by DUKE ELLINGTON
and BOB RUSSELL

27

DON'T GET AROUND MUCH ANYMORE

from SOPHISTICATED LADY

Words and Music by DUKE ELLINGTON
and BOB RUSSELL

I GOT IT BAD AND THAT AIN'T GOOD

Words by PAUL FRANCIS WEBSTER
Music by DUKE ELLINGTON

I LET A SONG GO OUT OF MY HEART

Words and Music by DUKE ELLINGTON,
HENRY NEMO, JOHN REDMOND
and IRVING MILLS

I'M BEGINNING TO SEE THE LIGHT

featured in SOPHISTICATED LADIES

Words and Music by DON GEORGE,
JOHNNY HODGES, DUKE ELLINGTON
and HARRY JAMES

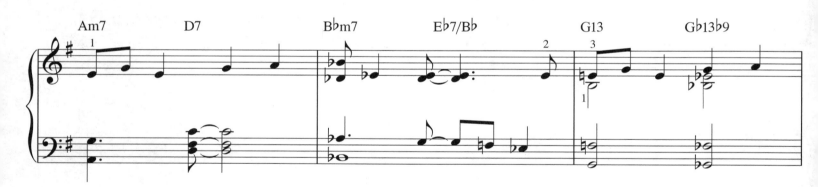

IN A MELLOW TONE

By DUKE ELLINGTON

48

IN A SENTIMENTAL MOOD

By DUKE ELLINGTON

IT DON'T MEAN A THING
(If It Ain't Got That Swing)
from SOPHISTICATED LADIES

Words and Music by DUKE ELLINGTON
and IRVING MILLS

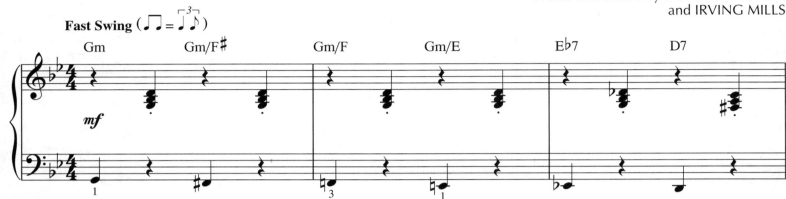

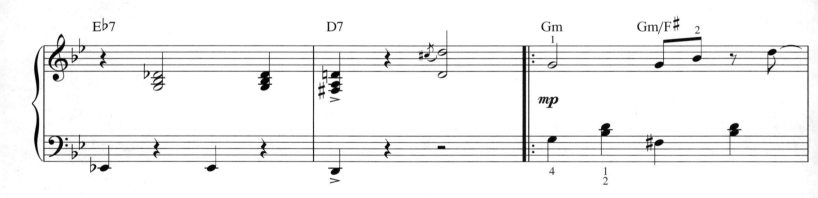

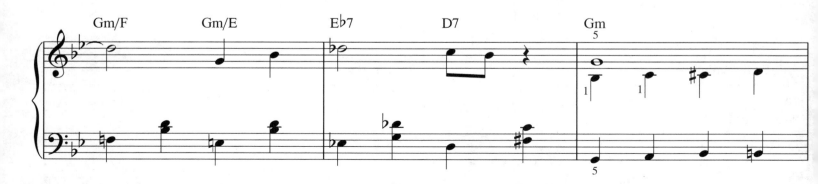

LOVE YOU MADLY

By DUKE ELLINGTON

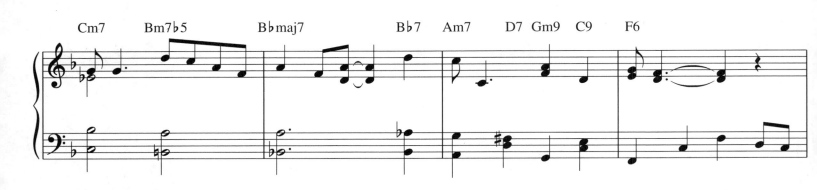

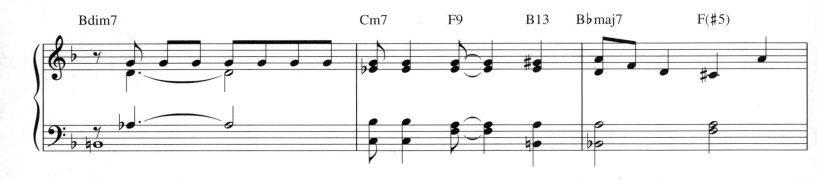

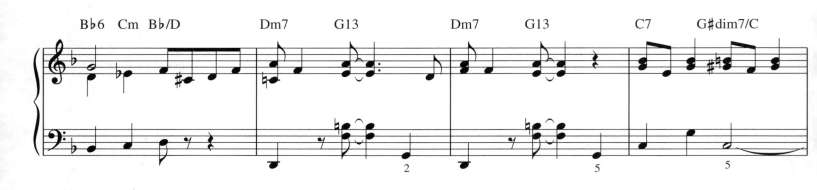

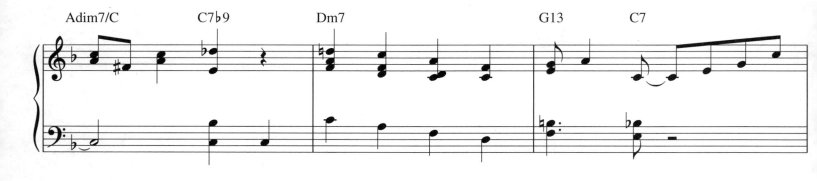

JUST SQUEEZE ME
(But Don't Tease Me)

Words by LEE GAINES
Music by DUKE ELLINGTON

MOOD INDIGO
from SOPHISTICATED LADIES

Words and Music by DUKE ELLINGTON,
IRVING MILLS and ALBANY BIGARD

PRELUDE TO A KISS

Words by IRVING GORDON and IRVING MILLS
Music by DUKE ELLINGTON

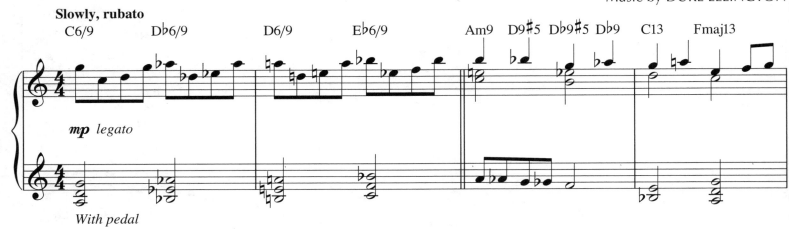

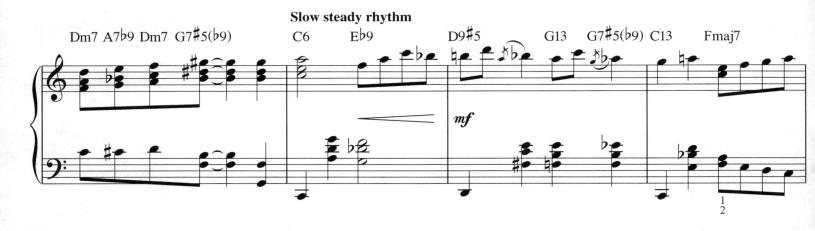

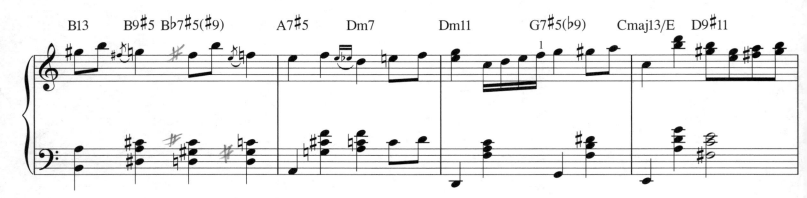

SATIN DOLL
from SOPHISTICATED LADIES

By DUKE ELLINGTON

72

SOLITUDE

Words and Music by DUKE ELLINGTON
EDDIE DE LANGE and IRVING MILLS

SOPHISTICATED LADY
from SOPHISTICATED LADIES

Words and Music by DUKE ELLINGTON,
IRVING MILLS and MITCHELL PARISH

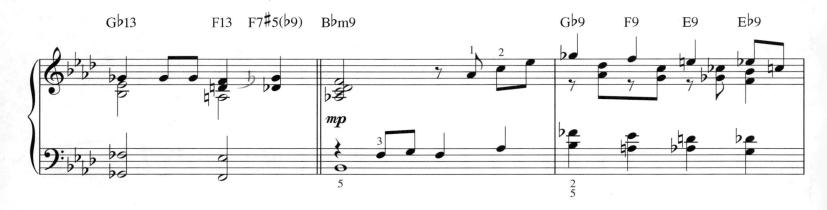

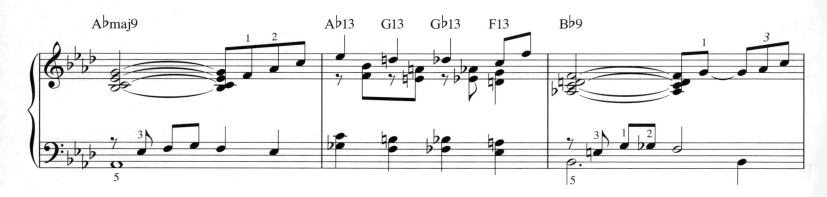

TAKE THE "A" TRAIN

Words and Music by
BILLY STRAYHORN

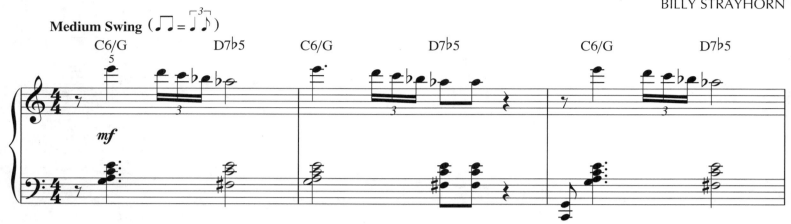

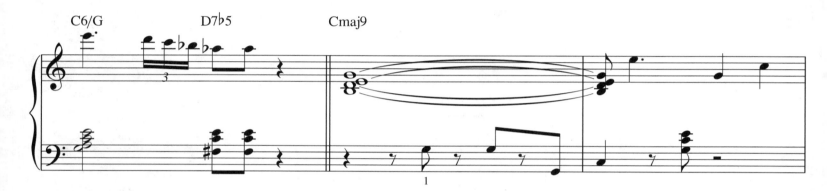

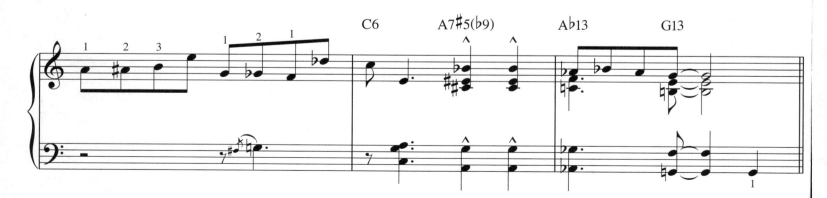

THINGS AIN'T WHAT THEY USED TO BE

By MERCER ELLINGTON

PERDIDO

Words by HARRY LENK
and ERVIN DRAKE
Music by JUAN TIZOL

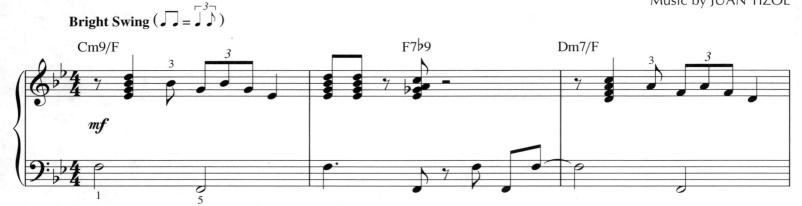

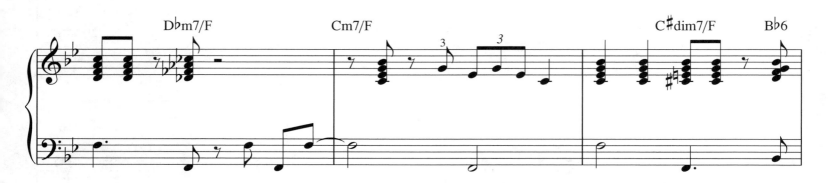

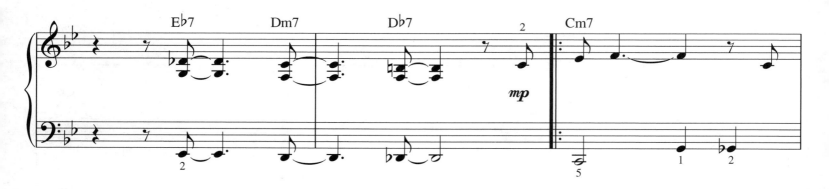

Buster Books

SHERLOCK BONES and the ADDITION & SUBTRACTION ADVENTURE

Illustrated by John Bigwood

(With additional illustrations by Dave Shephard)

Written by Jonny Marx and Kirstin Swanson

Edited by Jonny Marx

Designed by Jack Clucas and John Bigwood

Educational Consultancy by Kirstin Swanson

DOCTOR CATSON

SHERLOCK BONES

PROFESSOR MORIRATTY

My name is Sherlock Bones (world-class detective and professional calculation cracker). It is my job to solve conundrums using my superb maths skills and to catch cunning criminals when I can.

Can you help me in my Addition and Subtraction Adventure and track down my evil archenemy, Professor Moriratty, in the process? You will earn medals as you progress, and the puzzles will test different numeracy skills as you work your way through the book. My faithful accomplice, Dr Catson, and I are on board to offer you some helpful hints throughout.

You can use a piece of paper to jot down your workings.

2

BRONZE LEVEL
Elementary Addition

Catson and I use **addition** (+) to calculate a total.

This week, for instance, I have eaten 3 + 2 + 10 cans of dog food, which makes a whopping 15 cans in total. Solving crimes is hungry work!

Use your awesome addition skills to solve the following puzzles:

Write your answers in the blank spaces and check them at the back of the book.

PUZZLE 1

Catson is about to promote some of the cadet cats and dogs. She needs to **count** how many police badges are in the stock room. Can you help her calculate the **total**?

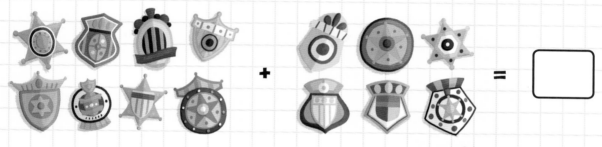

+ ... **=** ☐

PUZZLE 2

OH NO! There has been a robbery at Mrs Moo's shop. Can you **add up** the cost of the stolen items to calculate the **total**?

£3 **+** £5 **+** £10

The **total** cost of the stolen items is **£**

If you get stuck adding more than two numbers together, try and break the sum into sections, like so:

3 + 7 + 11 = ?
3 + 7 = 10
and 10 + 11 = 21

PUZZLE 3

Is the statement below **TRUE** or **FALSE**?

Adding together two **odd** numbers **ALWAYS** creates an **even** number.

The answer is ☐

PUZZLE 4

Catson has been dusting for prints at the crime scene. She's been using different colours (**blue**, **green**, **red** and **yellow**) for different animals. How many paw prints did she find altogether?

How many **blue** prints are there? ☐

How many **green** prints are there? ☐

Add the **blue** and **green** prints together. What is the **total**? ☐

How many **red** prints are there? ☐

How many **yellow** prints are there? ☐

Add the **red** and **yellow** prints together. What is the **total**? ☐

QUICKFIRE QUIZ 1

5 + 2 = ☐   7 + 6 = ☐   9 + 3 = ☐

6 + 5 = ☐   8 + 4 = ☐   6 + 4 = ☐

12 + 9 = ☐   21 + 10 = ☐   17 + 4 = ☐

13 + 5 = ☐   36 + 11 = ☐   43 + 10 = ☐

Simple Subtraction

Catson and I use **subtraction** (−) to take away from a number.
On Monday, for example, Dr Catson bought 4 cans of cat food and she ate 3 of them. We can, therefore, work out that Catson only has 1 can left:

    −   =

Use your superb subtraction skills to solve the following puzzles:

PUZZLE 5

Catson and I have followed some of Moriratty's gang into the sewers, but several of the rungs on the ladders are missing. Can you use your super subtraction skills to help us get to the bottom of each ladder safely?

LADDER 1
Should have
10 rungs

LADDER 2
Should have
15 rungs

LADDER 3
Should have
20 rungs

3 rungs missing

This puzzle can be written as
10 − 3 = ?

7 rungs missing

6 rungs missing

How many rungs are left on the ladder? ☐

How many rungs are left on the ladder? ☐

How many rungs are left on the ladder? ☐

PUZZLE 6

Success! We've found one of Moriratty's safe houses. Catson has been watching the property for some time. She saw **50** rats enter the house. After that, **26** left, followed by a further **19**. How many rats remain in the house?

The answer is

50

PUZZLE 7

Pablo Pollock had two paintings in his gallery. The pictures were collectively worth **£50** in total. One of the paintings was stolen by a mystery thief. The stolen painting was worth **£13**. What is the value of the remaining painting?

The answer is

£

QUICKFIRE QUIZ 2

9 – 5 = ☐   12 – 7 = ☐   15 – 13 = ☐

17 – 7 = ☐   18 – 5 = ☐   28 – 6 = ☐

33 – 4 = ☐   46 – 8 = ☐   58 – 9 = ☐

51 – 10 = ☐   65 – 30 = ☐   83 – 21 = ☐

Nifty Number Bonds

This is a **number bond.** It shows the relationship between numbers when you add or subtract from them.

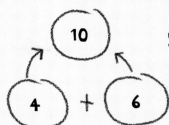

By looking at this number bond, you can determine the following:

That ... $4 + 6 = 10$
That ... $10 - 6 = 4$
That ... $10 - 4 = 6$

In order to be a world-class detective, your mental agility has to be lightning quick. Use your number knowledge to work out the missing numbers in this puzzle section.

PUZZLE 8

Catson and I use number bonds to crack cases.
Can you crunch the numbers and find the answers?

Here's an example of a puzzle that has been completed.

50
22 + 28

a) ◯
10 + 9

b) ◯
6 + 7

c) 23
◯ + 4

d) 22
15 + ◯

e) ◯
17 + 10

f) ◯
25 + 12

g) ◯
8 + 3

i) ◯

+

h) ◯
14 + 6

PUZZLE 9

Dr Catson and I think we may have uncovered one of Professor Moriratty's secret hideouts. However, in order to crack the access code for the door, we need to solve the puzzle. Put your number skills to the test to gain the correct code.

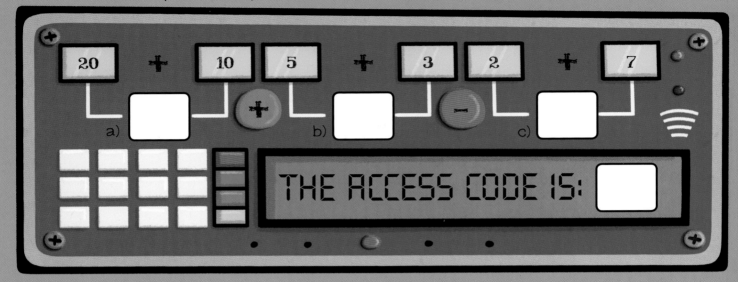

PUZZLE 10

Catson thinks Moriratty's gang has been using a network of sewer systems to commit some of their crimes. She has noticed that they enter and exit using different manhole covers, the sum of which always adds up to **100**. If, for example, the gang entered a manhole with the number **20** on it, the other end would have **80** on it. Can you trace the routes of the rats and work out which number should appear on each cover?

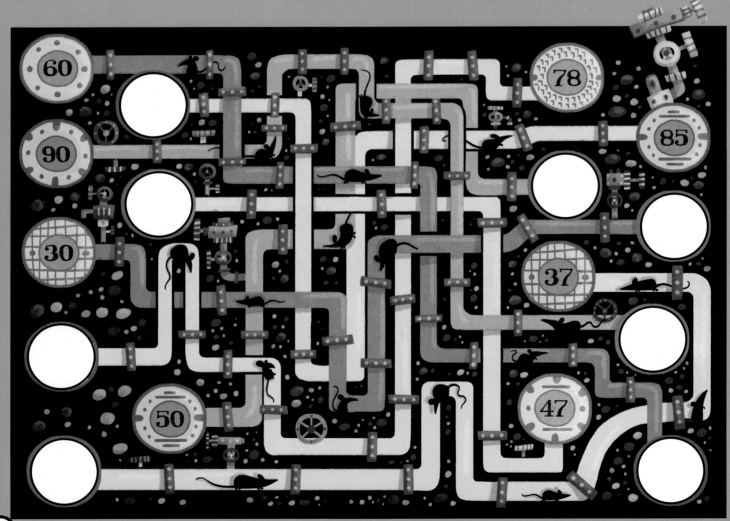

PUZZLE 11

A purse was reported stolen a few days ago. Catson and I raced to the scene of the crime, but could not catch the culprit. A few days later, the purse was handed in to the police station by an anonymous mouse. Curious indeed!

The victim said that the purse had £90 in it. Take a look at the evidence and see if you can solve the sums.

EVIDENCE

How much money is left?

£ [ ]

How much was stolen?

£ [ ]

MORIRATTY MISCHIEF
BRONZE

Someone has stolen the Diamond of Digits from the National Museum of Priceless Artefacts. The diamond was on display atop the Pyramid of Peril. We suspect Professor Moriratty may have been up to his dirty tricks again, but we need to scale the pyramid in order to dust for paw prints.

Can you solve the puzzle below to earn your **BRONZE**-level medal?

The blocks work in the same way as number bonds. The numbers in blocks next to one another can be added together to equal the number in the block above them. In the middle of the bottom row, for example, 8 + 6 = 14.

The number in the **green brick** is [ ]

The number in the **red brick** is [ ]

The number in the **yellow brick** is [ ]

?

?   ?

17   14   9

?   8   6   ?

To solve the yellow brick, you will have to work out which numbers belong in the two bricks beneath it.

SILVER LEVEL
Crazy Column Puzzles

Column puzzles are useful when you want to add or subtract big numbers. You must start by first solving the **ONES COLUMN** (on the right-hand side). Then you can move on to the **TENS COLUMN**.

```
  T  O

  8  2
+ 1  7
-------
  9  9
```

Dr Catson has been cracking some addition and subtraction calculations. However, she has since discovered that some of the numbers have vanished. She must have been using the invisible ink by mistake! Can you deduce what numbers are missing in the following problems?

If the numbers in the **ONES COLUMN** add up to ten or above, you will need to carry a '1' across to the **TENS COLUMN**. This is called REGROUPING as we have REGROUPED ten ones into one ten.

PUZZLE 1: ADDITION

a)
```
  3 [ ]
+ 4  7
------
  7  9
```

b)
```
  6  5
+ 2  3
------
  8 [ ]
```

c)
```
  5  7
+ 1  4
------
  7 [ ]
```

d)
```
[ ] 6
+ 4  6
------
  9  2
```

e)
```
  5  2
+[ ] 8
------
  7  0
```

f)
```
  7  1
+ 2  6
------
[ ] 7
```

When you carry a number over, it can help to write it in at the bottom of the tens column so you don't forget it.

INVISIBLE INK

PUZZLE 2: SUBTRACTION

If you cannot subtract the numbers in the **ONES COLUMN** (because the second number is bigger than the first), you'll have to borrow from the digit in the **TENS COLUMN**. Again, this is called REGROUPING. This time we are REGROUPING one ten into ten ones.

a)
```
  8 [ ]
- 5 2
-----
  3 6
```

b)
```
  5 9
- 3 6
-----
[ ] 3
```

c)
```
  4 2
- 2 3
-----
[ ] 9
```

d)
```
  6 5
- 4 [ ]
-----
  1 8
```

e)
```
  T  O
  2  3
- 1  8
------
  0 [ ]
```

PUZZLE 3

a) Now, can you ADD together all of the missing numbers in **PUZZLE 1**?

The **TOTAL** is [ ]

b) Now, can you ADD together all of the missing numbers in **PUZZLE 2**?

The **TOTAL** is [ ]

c) To prove that you are a SILVER-level puzzle solver, can you subtract the **PUZZLE 2** total from the **PUZZLE 1** total?

The **ANSWER** is [ ]

Formidable Fractions

Catson and I use **fractions** when trying to work out how much of something is left. This morning, for example, I left $\frac{5}{12}$ of my breakfast, and Catson left $\frac{1}{12}$. In total, we left $\frac{6}{12}$. This fraction can then be **simplified**. 6 and 12 can be divided by **6**, so $\frac{6}{12} = \frac{1}{2}$. When adding fractions with the same denominator (bottom number) you only add the numerators (top number) and the denominator stays the same.

PUZZLE 4

Dr Catson and I have been pursuing those pesky rats and we must be hot on their tails. We've found a hideout where they must have just been, because the food is still warm. Can you calculate the fractions of food that are left?

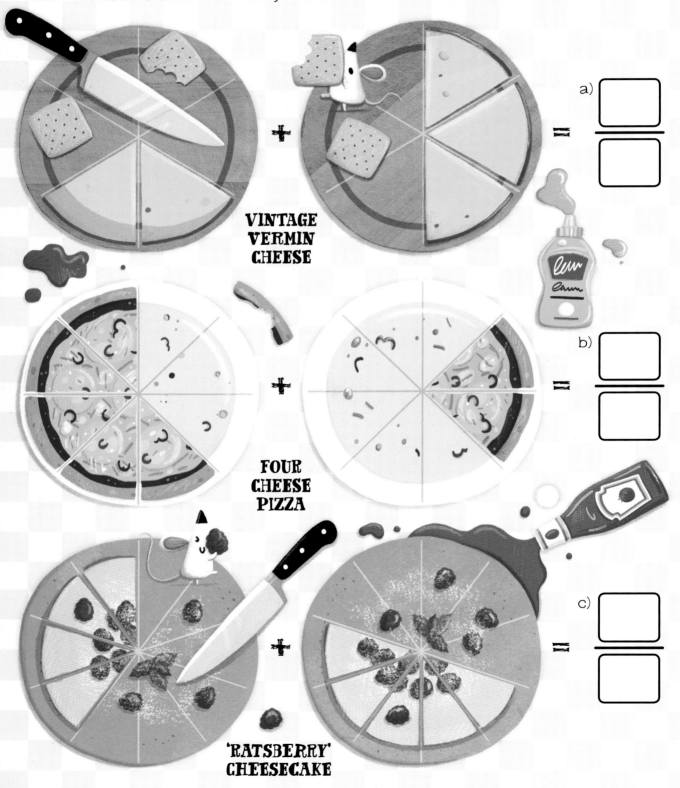

VINTAGE VERMIN CHEESE

FOUR CHEESE PIZZA

'RATSBERRY' CHEESECAKE

PUZZLE 5

We've been observing Moriratty's skyscraper, **PLAGUE TOWER**, on Wool Street. We want to raid the building when it is at its busiest. Can you work out what fraction of the lights are turned on at different times? The more lights, the busier the building. We're particularly interested in identifying which room is Moriratty's office so we can snoop around. It's never occupied, so the light is never on.

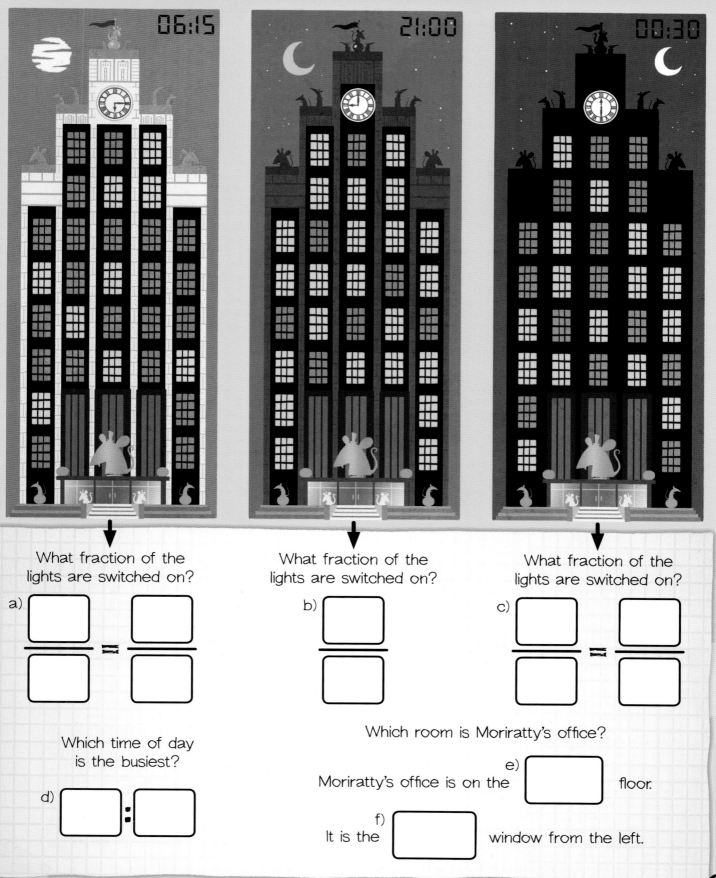

What fraction of the lights are switched on?

a) ☐/☐ = ☐/☐

What fraction of the lights are switched on?

b) ☐/☐

What fraction of the lights are switched on?

c) ☐/☐ = ☐/☐

Which time of day is the busiest?

d) ☐ : ☐

Which room is Moriratty's office?

e) Moriratty's office is on the ☐ floor.

f) It is the ☐ window from the left.

Money Magic

When adding or subtracting money, you must remember that there are 100 pennies (p) in a pound (£). The decimal point is always placed after the pounds, but before the pennies. **£7.25**, for example is just a better way of saying **725 pennies** — it's also much easier to fit in your pocket!

PUZZLE 6

My dear Catson has pointed out that my wardrobe could do with an update. Can you calculate how much it would cost me to buy the following items?

Hat £14.55

Cloak £7.25

The ANSWER is

£ [ ] . [ ]

PUZZLE 7

Now that I am looking tip-top, I thought I better invest in some new supplies. How much would it cost me to buy the following items?

Magnifying glass £8.20

Notebook £6.99

The ANSWER is

£ [ ] . [ ]

PUZZLE 8

Now, how much have I spent altogether?

£ [ ] . [ ]

PUZZLE 9

Catson is in charge of the kitty and gave me £50 to spend. How much change will I have to give back to her?

£ [ ] . [ ]

PUZZLE 10

Mrs Moo has called to say she's just made a suspicious sale in her shop. She thinks the customer may have been working for Moriratty, as he made some extremely peculiar purchases. How much did he spend?

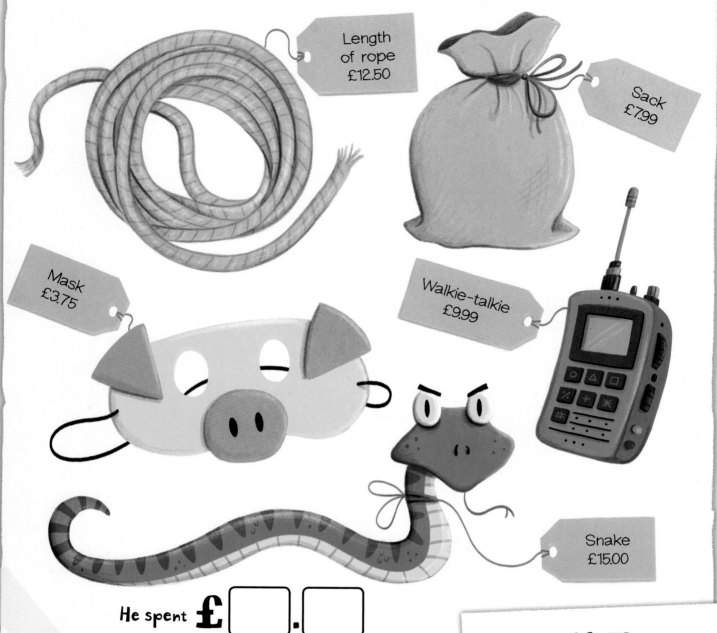

Length of rope £12.50

Sack £7.99

Mask £3.75

Walkie-talkie £9.99

Snake £15.00

He spent £ ☐ ☐ . ☐

£50

PUZZLE 11

The shifty shopper paid with a £50 note. How much change did he receive?

The ANSWER is

£ ☐ ☐ . ☐

QUICK TIP:

If you're struggling to work out the answer, you could try **ROUNDING** the numbers up or down and then adding or subtracting the difference. In **PUZZLE 7**, for instance, you could add £7.00 to £8.20 and then subtract £0.01.

TOP SECRET

CONFIDENTIAL

15

a)
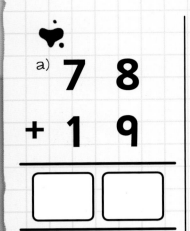

$$\begin{array}{r} 7\ 8 \\ +\ 1\ 9 \\ \hline \end{array}$$

b) 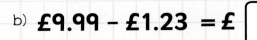 £9.99 – £1.23 = £ [ ]

c) $\frac{1}{10} + \frac{3}{10} + \frac{1}{10} =$ [ ]

d) $\frac{2}{7} + \frac{3}{7} + \frac{1}{7} =$ [ ]

e)

$$\begin{array}{r} 9\ 9 \\ -\ 4\ 3 \\ \hline \end{array}$$

[ ] [ ]

MORIRATTY MISCHIEF
SILVER

Just as we suspected, the Pyramid of Peril was covered in rat-sized paw prints. Catson and I were making our way back to the police station to file our report when a rushing rodent scurried right in front of us and dashed down an alleyway. Unfortunately, we weren't quite quick enough to catch the crafty creature. However, in all the chaos, we did find some dropped letters bearing Moriratty's wax seal. We've been trying to decode them ever since.

Can you use your addition and subtraction skills to work out the house number and door code?

Dear Professor Moriratty,

Thank you for visiting me. I knew it was you straight away - I recognized the rat-ta-tat-tat on the door. Can you tell me the house number and the door code?

Pipsqueak

Dear Pipsqueak,

Lovely to see you, as always.

Thanks for the ratatouille. It was delicious.

With regards to the question you asked, that's easy:

The house number is $48 + \frac{1}{2} + \frac{1}{2} + 3 - 17$. It's on Squeak Street.

The door code is: $72 + 2 + \frac{3}{4} + 6 + 4 - \frac{3}{4} - 8$.

Kind regards,

Moriratty

The house number is [ ]

The door code is [ ]

16

Once we'd worked out the house number and door code, we raced towards Squeak Street, following a narrow pathway along the edge of the river. We could hear footsteps sprinting ahead of us, but couldn't see anyone through the darkness. We were chasing shadows and had to speed up our pursuit. All of a sudden, Catson spotted a shortcut across the river. Can you use your **SILVER**-level skills to lead us safely across and earn your medal?

You need to work out which number should appear in each stepping stone using your addition and subtraction skills. The lines linking the stones work in exactly the same way as number bonds.

This puzzle will test all of the number skills you've learned so far in the book.

16

$11\frac{1}{2}$

9

$5\frac{3}{4}$

2

£9.15

£

£5.40

GOLD LEVEL
Subtle Number Sequences

Number sequences are useful when we want to identify patterns and relationships between numbers. Look at the number sequence below, for example:

5, 10, 15, 20, 25, 30, 35, 40, 45 ...

If you're purr-fect at maths you may have noticed that the numbers increase in multiples of **5**. The next number in the sequence would be **50**.

PUZZLE 1

There has been a sudden sequence of burglaries across the city. I've begun to piece together the case, taking note of the numbers of the burgled houses. It looks as though the gangs are working their way up and down the streets in patterns. Can you work out which house number is next on the gang's hit list in each sequence?

The house numbers follow a pattern. The pattern on each street is different.

a) **DOGTOWN DRIVE**
7, 9, 11, [ ], 15

b) **ANTEATER AVENUE**
25, 50, [ ], 100, 125

c) **SQUIRREL SQUARE**
63, 60, 57, 54, [ ]

d) **CATSON CLOSE**

0.4   0.45   0.5   0.55   [ ]

e) **BARKER STREET**

90   81   72   [ ]   54

f) **LIZARD LANE**

$\frac{1}{2}$ 1 $1\frac{1}{2}$ 2   [ ]

PUZZLE 2

Professor Moriratty is very particular about his food. He likes his cheese wedges to be organized into triangles to create an unusual number sequence.

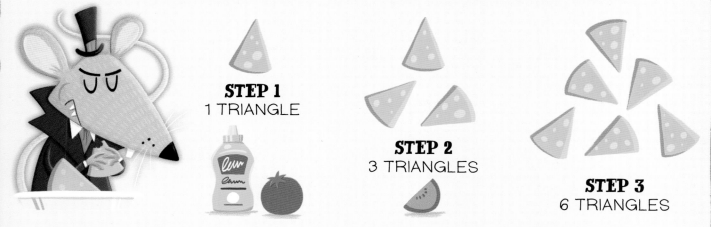

STEP 1
1 TRIANGLE

STEP 2
3 TRIANGLES

STEP 3
6 TRIANGLES

The numbers that are formed in this sequence are called triangle numbers.
How many triangles would be in the next three stages? Can you spot a pattern?

STEP 4
TRIANGLES

STEP 5
TRIANGLES

STEP 6
TRIANGLES

19

Nippy Negative Numbers
PUZZLE 3

Catson has been rooting through the evidence box again and she's pounced on an old thermometer. Unfortunately, some of the numbers have faded. Can you use the numbers that remain to identify the missing digits?

If you are already on a nippy negative number such as -10°C (bbrrr!) and you ADD, you will go UP the number line towards the positive number. If you think about it in terms of temperature, if you add more degrees, you will get WARMER.

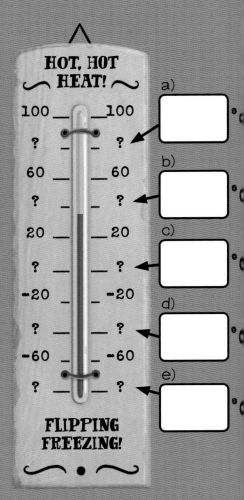

HOT, HOT HEAT!

100 __	__100	a)
? —	— ?	
60 __	__60	b)
? —	— ?	
20 __	__20	c)
? —	— ?	
-20 __	__-20	d)
? —	— ?	
-60 __	__-60	e)
? —	— ?	

FLIPPING FREEZING!

PUZZLE 4

Mrs Moo is not a-moo-sed! Last night, someone cut the power to her shop and her stock is in danger of being ruined. This sounds like sabotage and I bet I know who's behind it. Can you help her calculate the correct temperatures to save her stock?

a) **THE FRIDGE**:
Needs to be set at 11°C - 8°C = [ ] °C

b) **THE FREEZER**:
Needs to be set at -24°C + 6°C = [ ] °C

c) **THE SHOP**:
Needs to be set at 31°C - 9°C = [ ] °C

d) **THE OVEN**:
Needs to be set at 135°C + 45°C = [ ] °C

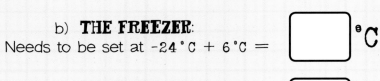

PUZZLE 5

We've teamed up with the **REALLY WILD WORLD POLICE** to uncover a series of Moriratty's secret hideouts across the globe. The hideouts are in different climates and we need to be prepared for the hot or cold weather when we arrive at each destination.

MOUNTAINS OF MISCHIEF
-2°C

VILLAINOUS VOLCANO
31°C

DEVILISH DESERT SANDS
51°C

EERIE ICE CAVES
-18°C

What is the temperature difference between the Mountains of Mischief and the Villainous Volcano?

a) ☐ °C

What is the difference in temperature between the Mountains of Mischief and the Eerie Ice Caves?

b) ☐ °C

Moriratty's sewers are 11°C. How much colder are the Eerie Ice Caves in °C?

c) ☐ °C

What is the temperature difference between the Mountains of Mischief and the Devilish Desert Sands?

d) ☐ °C

What is the difference in temperature between the Devilish Desert Sands and the Eerie Ice Caves?

e) ☐ °C

WORLD POLICE

21

Devilish Decimals

We use decimals to show small numbers. When comparing decimal numbers, always make sure you line them up carefully, so you can easily decide which is larger.

Here's an example:
0.2, 2.0, 0.02, 0.05

Now, if I look at the **ONES COLUMN**, I can see that the numbers here have a zero, apart from the second number from the top, which has a **2**. This means that this number is the LARGEST.

Next, I slide my paw across again to reveal the numbers in the **TENTHS COLUMN**. Aha! This time I can see they all have a zero, apart from the number at the top, which has a **2**. This means that this number is the next largest. If I continue this method, I can easily identify the largest and smallest numbers and easily write them in order.

If I stack decimal numbers on top of each other, I can look at each digit in turn.

0.2
2.0
0.02
0.05

ONES COLUMN

HUNDREDTHS COLUMN

TENTHS COLUMN

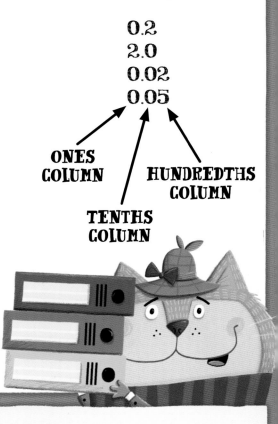

PUZZLE 6

I asked Catson to bring me all of the Moriratty case files. On the way back to the office, she tripped and fell down the stairs. Thanks to her incredible agility (and the fact she's a cat), Catson landed on her feet completely unharmed. All the case files, however, are now out of order. Can you help order the files for us into their separate colours? They need to be filed in numerical order, from largest to smallest.

YF 5.06

BF 2.1

GF 9.9

BF 2.6

YF 5.02

GF 9.09

YF 5.55

YF 5.0

GF 9.99

GF 9.0

BF 1.9

BF 2.0

BLUE files
(from largest to smallest):

YELLOW files
(from largest to smallest):

GREEN files
(from largest to smallest):

PUZZLE 7

We've been trying to crack a case for some time now and I've been stuck in the office for hours. I've sent Catson down to the canteen to get us something for lunch but I've only given her £5. Which options can she afford?

Menu

Hotdog – £3.45

Purr-fect pasta – £2.70

Pecked pigeon – £1.90

'Fee-line' pie – £4

Bottled water – £1.25

Carton of milk – 70p

OPTION 1:
Hotdog and a bottle of water.

OPTION 2:
Pecked pigeon and 'Fee-line' pie

OPTION 3:
Purr-fect pasta and a carton of milk

TOTAL:

£ _____

TOTAL:

£ _____

TOTAL:

£ _____

Can Catson afford this option?

_____

Can Catson afford this option?

_____

Can Catson afford this option?

_____

QUICKFIRE QUIZ 4

a) **21°C – 24°C =** ☐ **°C**

d) **2°C + 4°C =** ☐ **°C**

b) **8.20 + 1.40 – 9.60 =** ☐

e) **44°C – 35°C =** ☐ **°C**

c) **5.99 – 1.80 – 1.19 =** ☐

LOOKING AT THE ANSWERS, WHAT NUMBER WOULD APPEAR NEXT IN THE NUMBER SEQUENCE?

f) ☐

MORIRATTY MISCHIEF
GOLD

After crossing the river, Catson and I finally made our way to Squeak Street. We saw a rat tip-toeing towards the door. It was the very same shifty rat who'd scurried in front of us outside the museum. This had to be the house mentioned in Pipsqueak's letter. Could it be Professor Moriratty's fabled **MONSTROUS MANSION OF MYSTERY**? When the coast was finally clear, we carefully crawled over to the front door and typed in the access code. The huge lock flicked open and we hurried inside.

We found ourselves inside a vast entrance hall, surrounded by books. There was a note on a table in the centre of the room. Catson looked at it:

Dear Pipsqueak,

Bring the diamond to my secret vault. Just in case you've been followed, I've created a puzzling set of instructions only your clever brain will be able to comprehend.

To access the secret passage and open the door,
imagine you start with pounds twenty-four.
You purchase an item for £18.10,
(you may need to use a paper and pen).
You buy something else, it costs 60p,
and now my dear fellow, won't you kindly tell me,
with £24 you did start, and subtracted from the lot,
so how much money have you now got?

Once you've figured this out, find the book in my luxurious library with the matching number on its spine and give it a tug.

P.T.O.

The book number is ☐☐.☐

Once we found the book, Catson pulled it from the shelf. We heard a big thud, but nothing moved. We couldn't work out what had gone wrong and spent the next hour wasting precious time looking for more clues. It was only then that Catson had the bright idea of looking at the other side of the letter.

Now find the thermostat and take off the cover. It's behind the book by Shrill Snakespeare — the one about star-crossed lovers.

Look at the temperature, it's a chilly minus 7. I like my house cold, but turn up the heat by 11.

Now look at the sequence below and work out the missing number:

1.25, 1.5, 1.75, ?

Add this hidden figure to the temperature total to open the door, asunder.

Regards,

Moriratty

Can you solve Moriratty's temperature test to earn your **GOLD**-level medal?

The thermostat should be set to ☐ °C

PLATINUM LEVEL
Different Denominators

We can only add and subtract fractions with the same denominators (the number on the bottom of each fraction: the 2 in $\frac{1}{2}$, for example, or the 4 in $\frac{1}{4}$). If we are trying to add and subtract fractions with different denominators, we **MUST** convert them so that they are the same. Take a look at the fractions below, for example:

$$\frac{2}{5} + \frac{3}{10}$$

We cannot add fifths and tenths. However, we can use our multiplication knowledge and see that 10 is a multiple of 5 and if I multiply 5 by 2, I make 10. Therefore, I have to multiply my first fraction by two:

$$\frac{2}{5} \begin{array}{c} \times 2 \\ \times 2 \end{array} = \frac{4}{10}$$

$\frac{4}{10}$ and $\frac{2}{5}$ are **EQUIVALENT**, meaning they are the same, but I can now add $\frac{4}{10}$ to $\frac{3}{10}$ which would give me $\frac{7}{10}$. Sometimes, our answers can be simplified by dividing the numerator and denominator by the same number. For example, $\frac{6}{10}$ can be broken down into $\frac{3}{5}$.

PUZZLE 1

Can you convert these denominators to solve the fraction problems below?

a) $\dfrac{2}{3} + \dfrac{1}{6} = \dfrac{\boxed{}}{\boxed{}}$

NOT ALL FRACTIONS CAN BE SIMPLIFIED.

b) $\dfrac{12}{20} - \dfrac{2}{10} = \dfrac{\boxed{}}{\boxed{}}$ Which can then be simplified to: $\dfrac{\boxed{}}{\boxed{}}$

c) $\dfrac{1}{4} + \dfrac{7}{12} = \dfrac{\boxed{}}{\boxed{}}$ Which can then be simplified to: $\dfrac{\boxed{}}{\boxed{}}$

d) $\dfrac{20}{30} - \dfrac{2}{5} = \dfrac{\boxed{}}{\boxed{}}$ Which can then be simplified to: $\dfrac{\boxed{}}{\boxed{}}$

PUZZLE 2

Mrs Moo is going to throw an elaborate dinner party. She has invited lots of her friends, including me and Catson. She needs to work out how much food to buy, based on how much she expects us all to eat. Can you add the quantities of all 6 guests to work out the total for each course?

JOT DOWN YOUR WORKINGS ON A PIECE OF PAPER IF YOU NEED TO.

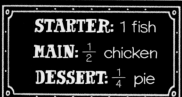

STARTER: 1 fish
MAIN: $\frac{1}{2}$ chicken
DESSERT: $\frac{1}{4}$ pie

STARTER: $\frac{1}{2}$ fish
MAIN: $\frac{1}{8}$ chicken
DESSERT: $\frac{1}{8}$ pie

STARTER: $2\frac{1}{2}$ fish
MAIN: $\frac{1}{4}$ chicken
DESSERT: $\frac{1}{8}$ pie

STARTER: $2\frac{1}{4}$ fish
MAIN: $\frac{1}{2}$ chicken
DESSERT: $\frac{3}{8}$ pie

STARTER: $3\frac{3}{4}$ fish
MAIN: $\frac{5}{8}$ chicken
DESSERT: $\frac{1}{8}$ pie

STARTER: 1 fish
MAIN: 1 chicken
DESSERT: 1 pie

How many fish does Mrs Moo need to buy?

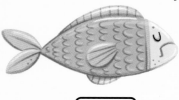

How many chickens does Mrs Moo need to buy?

How many pies does Mrs Moo need to buy?

Awesome Algebra

Algebra simply replaces a number with a letter. It really is as simple as that! Look at the puzzle below for example:

$$8 + m = 23$$

We can work out the value of m by adding upwards from 8 to make 23, or by subtracting 8 from 23, exactly like we did in the Nifty Number Bonds section.

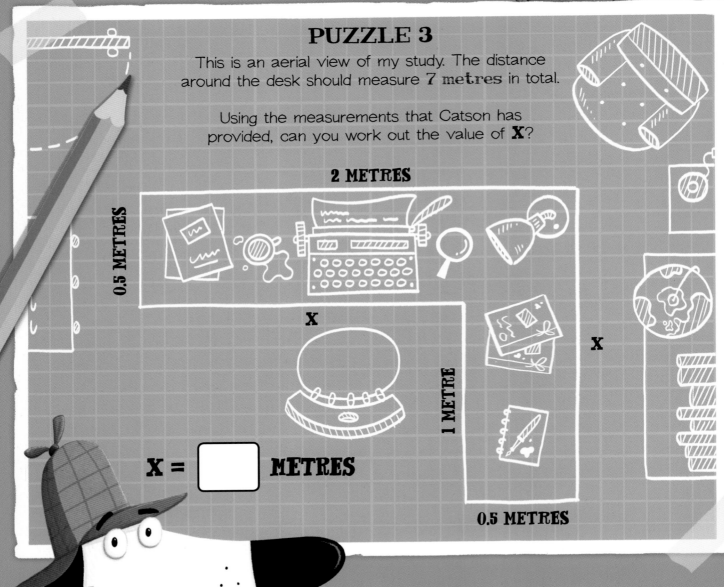

PUZZLE 3

This is an aerial view of my study. The distance around the desk should measure 7 metres in total.

Using the measurements that Catson has provided, can you work out the value of **X**?

2 METRES

0.5 METRES

X

1 METRE

X

X = ☐ **METRES**

0.5 METRES

To solve an algebra puzzle, you might need to use something called the **INVERSE** to work out the value of the letter. For example, if I had $14 + k = 20$, I could use the inverse and subtract instead. $20 - 14 = 6$. This gives me my answer because $14 + 6 = 20$.

28

PUZZLE 4

Catson and I are desperate to raid one of Moriratty's safe houses. Before we can begin, however, we have to study the blueprints of the building. The building was designed years ago, so some of the measurements have worn off. Can you use your addition and subtraction knowledge to calculate the value of each letter?

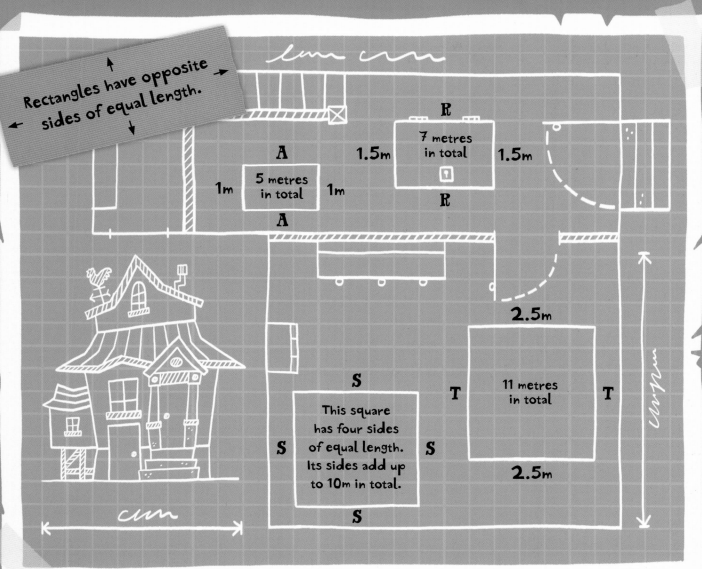

Rectangles have opposite sides of equal length.

A — 5 metres in total — **A**
1m — 1m

R — 7 metres in total — **R**
1.5m — 1.5m

S — This square has four sides of equal length. Its sides add up to 10m in total. — **S**

T — 11 metres in total — **T**
2.5m — 2.5m

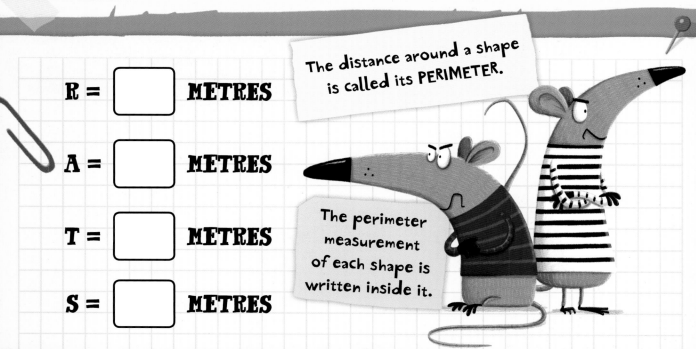

R = ☐ METRES

A = ☐ METRES

T = ☐ METRES

S = ☐ METRES

The distance around a shape is called its PERIMETER.

The perimeter measurement of each shape is written inside it.

29

Radical Roman Numerals

Roman numerals were used long before our number system. Catson and I like to use them to keep us on our toes. It's a useful skill to have when deciphering number puzzles from a long time ago.

1 = I
2 = II
3 = III
4 = IV
5 = V
6 = VI
7 = VII
8 = VIII
9 = IX
10 = X
11 = XI
12 = XII
13 = XIII
14 = XIV
15 = XV
16 = XVI
17 = XVII
18 = XVIII
19 = XIX
20 = XX
21 = XXI
30 = XXX
40 = XL
50 = L
100 = C

PUZZLE 5

Professor Moriratty's right-hand rat has been in prison for a long time. He's been carving the days into the wall. Can you add up the total to calculate how many days he's been locked up? Use the chart on the left to help you. Once you've worked out the answer, try and write it as a Roman numeral.

VII + XIV + XXI
+ IV + C + XL
+ XVII

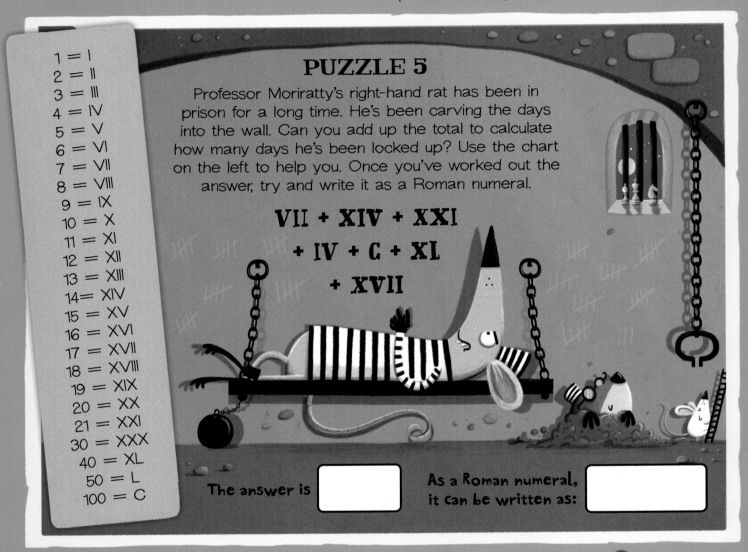

The answer is ☐

As a Roman numeral, it can be written as: ☐

QUICKFIRE QUIZ 5

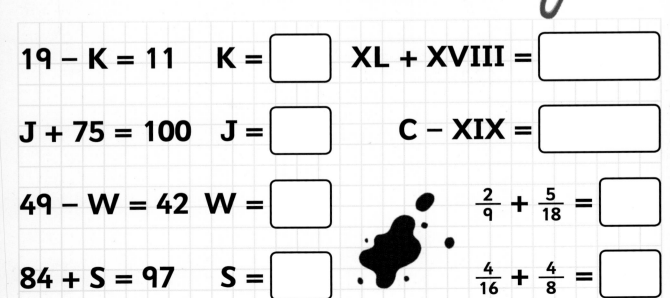

19 − K = 11   K = ☐   XL + XVIII = ☐

J + 75 = 100   J = ☐   C − XIX = ☐

49 − W = 42   W = ☐ $\frac{2}{9} + \frac{5}{18}$ = ☐

84 + S = 97   S = ☐ $\frac{4}{16} + \frac{4}{8}$ = ☐

MORIRATTY MISCHIEF   PLATINUM

Once Catson and I had set the thermostat to the right temperature, a panel in the bookcase moved, revealing a passageway. We bravely followed it into the depths of Moriratty's mansion. Can you follow the correct answers and lead us to Moriratty's bunker to catch the criminals and earn your Platinum Medal?

THE LARDER
The first room was filled with wheels of cheese – 18 to be exact! We were feeling a bit peckish, so Catson ate two of them, and I ate four. What fraction of the wheels did we eat in total?

$\frac{1}{3}$

THE GAMES ROOM
Catson and I got distracted by the snooker table. She potted 5/15 red balls and I potted 4/15. What fraction of the red balls did we pot in total?

$\frac{3}{5}$

$\frac{4}{7}$

THE LOUNGE
120 photos of Moriratty's friends and family are dotted around the lounge. Catson doodled on 37 of them, leaving the value Y untouched. What is the value of Y?

$\frac{1}{4}$

THE KITCHEN
There are 10 mice in the kitchen. 2/5 of them are cooking and 3/10 are washing up. What fraction of the mice are cooking or washing up?

OH NO! We've entered **LASER LANE**. Go back to **THE LARDER** and try your calculations again.

73   **83**

THE DINING ROOM
Moriratty's dining table is shaped like a cheese triangle. The total length around its three edges is 11.75 metres. Two of the edges measure 9.25 metres in total. What is the value of the missing edge?

$\frac{4}{5}$ **2.5M**

$\frac{7}{10}$

We've hit a dead end. Go back to **THE LARDER** and find a way through the mansion.

THE EPICENTRE
There are 24 CCTV cameras in Moriratty's mansion. 2/3 are spying on me, and 1/6 are focussing on Catson. How many cameras are observing us?

3.5M

Oh no! This path is blocked by lasers. Go back the other way.

XVIII

Wrong turn! Go back to the previous step.

XX

THE BUNKER

31

ANSWERS

Bronze

Puzzle 1
$8 + 6 = 14$

Puzzle 2
£18

Puzzle 3
True

Puzzle 4
Blue prints = 8
Green prints = 11
Blue + green = 19
Red prints = 10
Yellow prints = 9
Red + yellow = 19

Quickfire Quiz 1
$5 + 2 = 7$
$7 + 6 = 13$
$9 + 3 = 12$
$6 + 5 = 11$
$8 + 4 = 12$
$6 + 4 = 10$
$12 + 9 = 21$
$21 + 10 = 31$
$17 + 4 = 21$
$13 + 5 = 18$
$36 + 11 = 47$
$43 + 10 = 53$

Puzzle 5
Ladder 1 = 7
Ladder 2 = 8
Ladder 3 = 14

Puzzle 6
5

Puzzle 7
£37

Quickfire Quiz 2
$9 - 5 = 4$
$12 - 7 = 5$
$15 - 13 = 2$
$17 - 7 = 10$
$18 - 5 = 13$
$28 - 6 = 22$
$33 - 4 = 29$
$46 - 8 = 38$
$58 - 9 = 49$
$51 - 10 = 41$
$65 - 30 = 35$
$83 - 21 = 62$

Puzzle 8
a) 19
b) 13
c) 19
d) 7

e) 27
f) 37
g) 11
h) 20
i) 31

Puzzle 9
a) 30
b) 8
c) 9
Access code: 29

Puzzle 10
$60 + 40$
$15 + 85$
$90 + 10$
$53 + 47$
$30 + 70$
$22 + 78$
$50 + 50$
$63 + 37$

Puzzle 11
£18 left
£72 stolen

Bronze Medal
Green brick = 3
Red brick = 9
Yellow brick = 54

Silver

Puzzle 1
a) 2
b) 8
c) 1
d) 4
e) 1
f) 9

Puzzle 2
a) 8
b) 2
c) 1
d) 7
e) 5

Puzzle 3
a) 25
b) 23
c) 2

Puzzle 4
a) $5/6$
b) $7/8$
c) $9/10$

Puzzle 5
a) 06:15: $9/30 = 3/10$
b) 21:00: $23/30$
c) 00:30: $15/30 = 1/2$

d) The busiest time of day is 21:00

e) Moriratty's office is on the 8th floor

f) It is the 2nd window from the left

Puzzle 6
£21.80

Puzzle 7
£15.19

Puzzle 8
£36.99

Puzzle 9
£13.01

Puzzle 10
£49.23

Puzzle 11
£0.77

Quickfire Quiz 3
a) $78 + 19 = 97$
b) £9.99 - £1.23 = £8.76
c) $1/10 + 3/10 + 1/10 = 1/2$
d) $2/7 + 3/7 + 1/7 = 6/7$
e) $99 - 43 = 56$

Silver Medal
The house number is: 35

The door code is: 76

Stepping stone puzzle
4 $1/2$, 2 $1/2$, 3 $1/4$, 3 $3/4$, £3.75

Gold

Puzzle 1
a) 13
b) 75
c) 51
d) 0.6
e) 63
f) 2 $1/2$

Puzzle 2
Step 4 = 10
Step 5 = 15
Step 6 = 21

Puzzle 3
a) 80°C
b) 40°C
c) 0°C
d) -40°C
e) -80°C

Puzzle 4
a) 3°C
b) -18°C
c) 22°C
d) 180°C

Puzzle 5
a) 33°C
b) 16°C
c) 29°C
d) 53°C
e) 69°C

Puzzle 6
Blue = 2.6, 2.1, 2.0, 1.9
Yellow = 5.55, 5.06, 5.02, 5.0
Green = 9.99, 9.9, 9.09, 9.0

Puzzle 7
Option 1 = £4.70, Yes
Option 2 = £5.90, No
Option 3 = £3.40, Yes

Quickfire Quiz 4
a) 21°C - 24°C = -3°C

b) 8.20 + 1.40 - 9.60 = 0

c) 5.99 - 1.80 - 1.19 = 3

d) 2°C + 4°C = 6°C

e) 44°C - 33°C = 9°C

f) 12 would appear next in the sequence

Gold Medal
The book number is 5.30

The thermostat should be set to 6°C

Platinum

Puzzle 1
a) $2/3 + 1/6 = 5/6$

b) $12/20 - 2/10 = 8/20 = 2/5$

c) $1/4 + 7/12 = 10/12 = 5/6$

d) $20/30 - 2/5 = 8/30 = 4/15$

Puzzle 2
Fish = 11
Chickens = 3
Pies = 2

Puzzle 3
X = 1.5 m

Puzzle 4
R = 2 m
A = 1.5 m
T = 3 m
S = 2.5 m

Puzzle 5
The answer is 203
As a roman numeral CCIII

Quickfire Quiz 5
K = 8
J = 25
W = 7
S = 13
XL + XVIII = LVIII (58)
C - XIX = LXXXI (81)
$2/9 + 5/18 = 1/2$
$4/16 + 4/8 = 3/4$

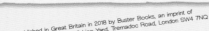
First published in Great Britain in 2018 by Buster Books, an imprint of
Michael O'Mara Books Limited, 9 Lion Yard, Tremadoc Road, London SW4 7NQ

This revised edition published in 2020

Copyright © Buster Books 2018, 2020

 www.mombooks.com/buster Buster Books @BusterBooks

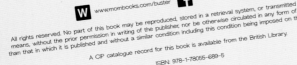
A CIP catalogue record for this book is available from the British Library.

ISBN: 978-1-78055-689-5

1 3 5 7 9 10 8 6 4 2

This book was printed in January 2020 by Leo Paper Products Ltd, Heshan Astros Printing Limited,
Xuantan Temple Industrial Zone, Gulao Town, Heshan City, Guangdong Province, China.